MW00905776

POURING SMALL FIRE

POURING SMALL FIRE

SUSAN MANCHESTER

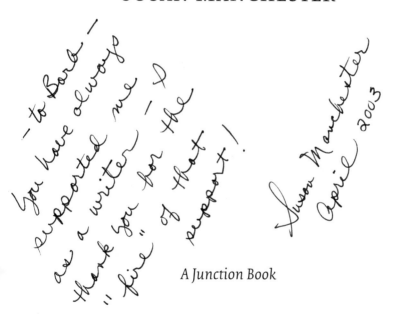

— to Barb —
You have always
supported me
as a writer — I
thank you for the
"fire" of that
support!

Susan Manchester
April 2003

A Junction Book

NIGHTWOOD EDITIONS

ROBERTS CREEK, BC

2003

Copyright © Susan Manchester, 2003

ALL RIGHTS RESERVED. The use of any part of this publication reproduced, transmitted in any form or by any means, electronic, mechanical, photocopying, recording, or otherwise, or stored in a retrieval system, without the prior written consent of the publisher—or, in the case of photocopying or other reprographic copying, a licence from the Canadian Copyright Licensing Agency—is an infringement of the copyright law.

Nightwood Editions
R.R. #22, 3692 Beach Ave.
Roberts Creek, BC
V0N 2W2, Canada

We gratefully acknowledge the support of the Canada Council for the Arts and the British Columbia Arts Council for our publishing program.

NATIONAL LIBRARY OF CANADA CATALOGUING IN PUBLICATION DATA

Manchester, Susan, 1952-
Pouring small fire / Susan Manchester.

Poems.
"A junction book".
ISBN 0-88971-189-5

I. Title.
PS8576.A585P68 2003   C811'.6   C2003-910148-7
PR9199.4.M35P68 2003

*To the parade of feelings created by others in me
and to the infinite shapes of all imagery,
I dedicate this small portion of who I am becoming.*

CONTENTS

ONE

Begin to fall forever back in one week's time
when time itself slides behind the lazy sun
when the sun loves shadows of leaves more
than fallen leaves themselves. Begin to fall back
back to dinner in frightened five o'clock darkness
the same darkness that brought father home
to a home in Camden where he staggered cold
from the dusk, cold from too many cigarettes, warm

from the beer, warm from the whisky, or the wine
the wine which made his breath sour. Begin,
begin to find that lost hour when mother
told you, mother swore, he spoke that way
that slurring way, because he had a cold
because his cold made him wheeze, because
because. Begin to use that hour, when he wore
that red wool jacket, wore that black hat, to remember what

he looked like, what he sounded like: "I'm fi-i-ine!"
          Begin.
"Re-e-eally!" Begin to add. "What's wrong with y-o-o-u?"
          Begin.
Begin to add the hours, one hour for each year
each year more distant, and find only a day-and-a-half
          missing.

FATHER BUILT A WALL

Thirty years ago, Father began to dig
into the side of Preston Hill using a pick

to break the sod that clung long and hard.
Rocks he tossed away fell heavy on the land.

And with each twilight thud the earth became
more and more deboned until the sun went down

and he came in to dinner. Soap could never
clean away the dirt those hands had held.

And as he ate, Mother felt the rhythm of the wall
with each forkful thrust into his mouth.

Until one night she thought the wall complete,
the garden safe, the snakes secure in shadow.

But with the day his hands took up the pick
again to split another clot of dirt,

as if by crumbling one more lump in earth's
chest and stacking one more stone he could

bleed the soil of all desire to sink
into the future.

Today she kicked the grass
and found a shoulder trying to break the surface,

a cornerstone with subtle pulse that would
not yield to level ground beneath her feet.

And out from under that sagging hill an arm
begins to reach at dusk, a hand begins

to pull her back to where the sound of pick
and shovel chipped away at time. But only

 when the grass grew tired of holding down
the rocks that arched their backs near her

did she begin to think that even snakes
know how to shed what they no longer need.

Almost a suction when they dive under the beam
from our flashlights. We lunge after night crawlers,
hands and fingernails black with dirt, trying to pull
them from the ground. They lie like miniature whales,
beached on wet grass. Dad perseveres, teaches us
that quick hands are not always enough
and we listen carefully, as if we understand the weight
of his teaching, when all we really understand
is his being with us in the dark, his hands upon
our hands, teaching, always teaching.

And night speaks to us and tells us we are right
to pursue worms, that the very hinge of the world's
door rides on the capture of these beasts. And
we believe their diving produces waves felt
on distant shores, never believing any moment
will ever be more important. We are making history
and never think of using our catch, only hoarding it
and showing it to Freddy Tate or Eddie Snyder who've
never had so many worms. But these are so much more
than worms. They are the night, the hours.

GENERATIONS

I

I was at the game because there was
no money for a babysitter and I was eight
or nine and Daddy wasn't home.

That hot-dog-mustard smell filled my head.
I don't think I ever had one, just knew
they meant sunset, summer, popcorn, batted

balls. It felt good, this baseball.
Baseball was that town. Any business
worth your business sponsored

a team: Harden Furniture, VFW, Camden
Wire, IGA. Green and white, blue and
red, black and white, red and black.

My brother played second base when
he wasn't pitching or when the coach
decided he would play at all. Each

time he was selected we cheered, "Hey
Manchester, go man-eater, honey kid,
honey babe!" Always those words: "Hey

kid, hey babe, honey kid, honey babe!"
Inflection up on the second word, no one
exempt from the chant. Even when I

played behind the bleachers with other
brothers and sisters, I could hear
the calls from players and parents:

"... honey kid, hey babe, honey babe, way
to go!" If it was too quiet, the coach would
bellow, "Let's talk it up out there now, let's go!"

II

My brother played second base in Babe
Ruth league. I watched more then.
I was older and he was older and playing well

meant so much more. He hustled. When I was
away from the bleachers, off to the clump of trees
behind third base, I'd swing on the tire with

the others. Still I'd want to hear the wood on the
ball, chatter from the field, umpire's groan: "Baawll!"
triumphant: "Steeerriiike threee! You're Ouoot!"

III

I watched the Yankees and Baltimore with
my grandfather. He'd say, "Boy!" each time
the Orioles made a great play, or someone sang

the national anthem. "Boy!" and "Gee!" and
"Hah. Look at that! Those Yankees can't win
even for all their money! How 'bout that?"

IV

And I remember watching Yankees' defence
with my dad and "wowing" after Nettles,
or "geezing" after Dent, or "yupping" after

Randolph turned the double play. It's a
blood thing—that smell of hot dogs, language
from the field, Rizzuto's "Holy Cow!," ERA

for Gossage, brothers and sisters massing
behind bleachers, dust on the plate, tag on the bag.
I've never escaped it and never felt more free.

Bat on the ball, base on errors, ball against
leather, called third strike, cleats kicking dirt.
And the team doesn't matter, never did in the end.

AFTER SUMMER

for Laura Lush

Between the rows of corn my brother and Eddie
built a baseball diamond small enough for success.

I was a *ragged* child, little sister Susie,
called chopsticks-strikeout king.

Nothing insurmountable for the boys, I was banished
at sunset from the team, usurped by Freddie Tate.

Slow song of grass moaning as I cried and tripped
toward the house by way of the chicken coop.

Boys' crude calls from the field told me
I would never be anyone but girl and they knew it.

All of this mere practice for caregiver years
as a woman—years too long to count.

The stars' silver fillings gleamed their
broad-toothed smiles and I-told-you-so commentary,

or night's cavities floated *across the sky.*

Either way: *what's left?*

That *our bodies* define who we are or what
we believe from our own mouths,

that even summer can be swallowed by the night,
consumed by its own dark voices,

that *the blue curve of the earth* tries to slow
the digestion of our becoming what we must.

MY TOWN

after Stephen Dobyns

It happened once a week on Preston Street.
First Eddie Snyder pulled on Duffy's chain
to stop the dog from barking. I heard the growl
and ran to get my brother. "It's coming, Larry!"
Then we'd run halfway up the hill to Tate's,
where Freddy screamed, "Wait for me!" Back down
to gather Jeff and Greg, and Rusty from
the sandbox—the day August-full of cicadas.
And again, "It's coming!" and now we could hear it
so we stopped on Phinney's lawn to look up the hill,
our mouths opened, sweat overcoming us as
even the heat took up the call. Just then
Roxanne came out. "Do you see it? Shhhhh!
Head for the underpass!" So there we stood
in shade at last, more alive than tired, as old
Doc Peck's wagon rolled nearer. Rusty sneezed
and echoed. We laughed our nervous laughs. Heard
the horse's, clip clip, clip clip, clip clip. We smelled
the garbage, and feared the ancient wagon's creaks,
the cultures in that refuse, the horse's whinny—
our mothers telling us to leave the guy
alone, that garbage is only junk, that Doc
is really Dexter, that horses were not made
to haul our putrid trash, that poor is not
a show for kids to watch from summer shadows—
CLIP CLIP, CLIP CLIP, clip clip, clip clip, clip clip. . . .

ON "THE RED SOIL"

for Daniel Varoujan

It still smoulders, the red soil given you,
you, who are the voice in my dead father's
dreams as he works the earth, as he smashes
the face of his hoe into the shoulder of a

hill. Red soil harbours your fists, tiny
mounds pushed over crocuses, each crocus a hand
with a soul. Wireworms blind the potatoes,
father's heart louder under dirt than it ever

was in life. He reaches for you, for you who
suffered longer than any of us ever will. You
knew the soil would never stop oozing, that no
amount of spring perfumes the blood. What is it

we must entrust to the black squirrels who bathe
in the dust and bury what they will? How many
seeds will it take to feed the dead? As long as
you are there beneath the weeds, my father sleeps.

And the flying ants are swarming again
as they do from the ground under rock.
I spray poison as I must to wipe out the
memory of their swarming inside the house
on Maple Drive—that tiny place mother
thought would be her dream house—
that place built on a slab of rock.
It welcomed all manner of insects: spiders,
cinch bugs, and nests of ants. How did we
live there and not become one with a colony
of something? After my father died, mice
ate through the bread drawer as mother was
grieving and alone. I trapped them with
glue-filled plastic plates where they tired
slowly. I threw them in the garbage. "So
inhumane," someone said. What death is not?
No one visited much until Dad was dying.
A friend invited his Pentecostal minister
to come and speak in tongues—tongues
in the midst of insects under slabs failed
to save my father and I wondered what language

could save any of us. I swear the walls echoed
for days. He would look at me sideways
with prisoner-of-war-camp eyes and nod as if
he heard voices, and I'd nod back, happy
that he believed in echoes, our silent language
speaking louder than tongues. Now, I am a
universe away from that house and the languages
in it, but nothing can save me from the tug
I can't resist, the glimpse that makes me,
speaks to me, horrifies me with images
of flying ants swarming in an effort to take wing.

AUGUST EVE

Summer and the honeyed air
rises, falls—like a lover breathing.
The only sound, this slow breathing
from the high branches of the pines.

"Alone," P.K. Page

Dinner is over and light just
drizzles through the trees
after a six o'clock shower.
Cedars are soft through the
fence, tipped greener at their ends
than July remembers. There is sherry,
tart and bare, unforgiving of the
faint-hearted, stiff and cool.
But this too, I swallow as I dare

summer and the honeyed air

to leave this evening. A memory
was broken tonight. Nothing more
than Syracuse china—a platter of
the pattern like my father's cracked
coffee cup, that even now to touch
brings back some subtle weaving
of his taste with mine. Shattered
platter, falling from the grill
cannot stop moving, or leaving

rises, falls—like a lover breathing.

"It's OK," I say. "It's a dish, nothing
more." Now that's the truth. But
no amount of distance removes
a childhood. And I begin to steam
the corn. It's only small, but
water in the pot is heaving,
pushing up by sighs, the lid.
Air is rising and falling
the bubbles seething,

the only sound, this slow breathing.

So dinner is served. The steak
is gone. We eat before
the rain. We speak before
the food, the evening quiet,
sunset deserted. Somehow,
my father sends his signs —
something in the bend of the candle,
the face in the shadows. "It's
OK," I say. His voice unwinds

from the high branches of the pines.

The past changes when parents die:
it questions and blames me
for unfinished snowsuit Sundays
when I could have lingered longer
in a five o'clock kitchen—
when I might have loved more completely
the coal-stove heat in the Camden cold—
when I should have been more grateful
for the tingling journey back from numbness,
crisp cheeks sizzling
lead toes soaking
at last
in a warm water basin.
I sat, toboggan-weary
on paisley tile, beaded snow clinging
to Belva's mittens,
matted hair smelling
like the woods.
I was not thankful enough
for returning from the clump of trees
unbitten
by loneliness.

TWO

LEAVING THE POND

leaving was harder than being there
what we have not resolved is the coming home
where you might linger
where you might give us a sign that
you didn't mean to fade away
that you miss us, that it was all right for us to
go to Old Forge without you

that the pine trees were silently missing you too
that the mist still paused, still hung low
on the sand where you sat looking at the lake
where you wished you were, where a single boat
rowing toward you reminded you
of a skirting water spider you watched as a kid
when dusk was all the grey you'd ever known
where your passing was a mirror where we could see
ourselves dissolving, where the only reason you lived
as long as you did, was to see yourself
one more time on the face of the pond

THERE ARE THINGS ABOUT GRIEF I DID NOT KNOW:

that with the knowledge
of each new death in town
another wound is opened

that real tears fall only
after four months have passed

that when I check
mother's closets for thieves
I'm really looking
to see if your clothes are there

that mother is really only half-alive
and you are really only half-dead

that when my niece sits
in your place at the table
she is saving it for you

that the grass reminds me of you
because the rabbits are running across it
and you loved the rabbits

that the cushion in your chair
will always have the imprint
of your tailbone
worn through your skin

that your glasses are still
next to your Bible by your chair

that your keys lie
where you set them
when you came into the house
for the last time

that Old Forge might be
a place we can never enjoy seeing again

that all Cornell graduates
have something in common with you

that your razor and the little box I rescued
from the garbage the day after we buried you
are still on the sink

that your smell is all over that house

that you sit in mother's dreams
on the edge of her bed
telling her not to cry

that two weeks after you died
she felt your leg against hers in bed

that grief is the longest relationship
I will ever have with you.

MY PARENTS, DROWNING

father died like a rock falling through water
sinking deeper than weeds beneath
the surface of his breathing

or like a slow caution light seeking
red just before it rains.

my brother was there, my mother too, and we
stood as great blue herons in the mud,
our watch producing no fish to spear

only a glimpse of his eye's light fading

no questions then, just answers that covered
us in wet wool blankets, heavy reasonings, God
descending everywhere, carefully around us—

no distance between earth and heaven.

mother floats on the water now, lily pad
staring at the sun. she is to be pulled under
and soon, or dragged by a rock. father waits,
coughing up snails at the bottom of the pond.

UNDER MUD

it's all right to be blind

to chew sand and like it

to fill the nose with clay and suffocate

to cough up bits of toad, to savour algae

all right to wrap black around

the night and stay glued to the dark

all right to want to cry

to taste mud, to smell snail

all right to be so unseen

so used by the earth under the pond

so sure that no one will follow

that the sun stays away by choice

that the night claims all flesh

uses even hair to tie limbs together

Had raindrops like bouncing BBs
stopped dancing on the picnic table,

had a green-and-white-striped umbrella
not trotted across deaf sand,

had a restless motor not frayed
a ribbon of white foam,

had a sudden sigh not parted
leaves held against the sky,

had the relentless damp wanted
to prevent the passage of time,

my father would have seen a perfect
still life, the last time he saw Old Forge:

pond drenched grey-ash under mist,
its surface cut by sharp rain,

rigid poplar and birch resisting
the nudge of the breeze,

smoke sifted finely on spruce
over the south shore,

boats hitched and bedded down,
sky lined in grey flannel.

Had the relentless damp wanted
to prevent the passage of time.

Many of the images refuse to part,
dictions of light still make up the light,
the broken theories depart like the water,
though the water did not depart: it is just waiting,

"The Song Is Passing like a Wave," Michael Burkard

Universe at the bottom of the pond, what do you keep?
Mud answers no questions, takes the shine off all stones,
levels its language into one long moan in winter.
Those who are imagined there: thrown-over doll,
bullhead eyes, black boot, and snail shells — stay only
to please themselves. Someone anywhere sees art
in the muck, gives the doll's head fish eyes, paints
both legs in one boot, clasps a mollusc bracelet around
her wrist. Oh the joy in creation! The pictures a heart
can pour itself into. *Many of the images refuse to part,*

even after another painting entertains the time. Then
there's the lack of sun, where blindness is bliss or
merely motion. Weeds that wave, do so unseen but lose
no respect for their courage, their lack of knowledge.
Light would not help them recover stillness. And this
silent city speaks in rhythms only a deaf night
can hear. Algae cannot lie. Pebbles remember when
all life had gills and breathed in whispered elegance.
Must I admit weakness by forfeiting my sight?
I know *dictions of light still make up the light,*

still pull me away from the water I try to embrace.
If I descend, where do I find love? Its hands
like sand, kisses like air bubbles, breath as I
know it, denied? Can love be a quilt of scales?
Shall I lie my head on a lily pad, curl my toes
under groggy tree roots, sink out of sight later
when the shadows remind me that night swallows all?
The answer is always no. Returning, only
to know the origin of a species, matter,
light. *The broken theories depart like the water*

when a mirage melts. So it was that I was contained
on the face of the pond in a boat, or held by the
arm of the dock, or the belly of a raft. (I could
have patched an inner tube's eye to be closer to the
reeds on the north shore.) My longing was to drown,
to go where I could not go. Frogs sat huge, berating
me to follow sunbeams into the dark, to taste darkness
forever. I thought the night might follow me. I thought
the water would give way to dry land, disintegrating—
though the water did not depart: it is just waiting.

HARBOUR

this trust like white sand
cleaves to us
touching us to the sea

this trust that rolls
into the space
we share
pulling us like a wave
toward the same ocean

a wave away from this
harbour
toward any other
shore together

this harbour we leave
filled with the air
we breathed for
each other

UNDINE

Like glitter, blue-silver, from the lake

under morning's fingertips, you stroke dawn

dipping a toe into daylight. And when you

let the air receive you, your blush holds

the curious light in check. Your lips await

the sun's desire to paint them moist, flesh

on flesh to wet the tip of silence. And you

shudder the thought that makes you want

the earth to kiss your breast. You stay

only long enough to sift your soul upon the

rocks. It will not rest—that call from under

water's face. I watch you lean and sway

as if the end has come too soon. You fall

upon the stars and sink into the night.

THIS IS THE DREAM

to ride the current so finally
that even the fish whisper

to lose myself in stones
between crevices
in the creek

to disintegrate on the rocks
peacefully
until all that remains is my hair
until that too rolls patiently
away

to be so completely used

to touch every shore at the same time

THREE

you will say, "so soon?"
it will be after you blink
that I come stumbling to you
through some portal
you looking as surprised as
I was when you left.
and you will be certain that

this is "meant to be"
and you will tell all you've learned
and you will say how eternity leaves
no time for grief
no time for self-pity and certainly
no time for regret
and I will wonder how you learned
these things so fast.

you will not hug me.
you will take my hand and
lead me to mother who has just
opened her eyes too
and wonders why she feared leaving.
and we will continue waking forever.

The landscape is tossing things around: babies
riding in frying pans, a screwdriver through
the abdomen of a cocker spaniel stuck
on a window ledge, a bronze cross emerging
from the belly of a stuffed bear, a telephone
receiver working its way through an American
flag.
        I want bread,
want to set it to rise in mother's clay bowl. I
want dolls with heads attached, steering wheels
steering, hair combed, combs themselves.
I want to make love on dry land again,
when you were stable under me or in back
of me or on top of me. I want this to matter
again.
                 I want white,
yellow and pink. I want the end of night
on this planet, before the age of watermarks,
before everything was dipped in darker and
darker dye. I want my ear on the ground
to hear horses' hooves from a distance.
Want to be able to fall and scrape knees, to
bleed and see blood, to suffer concussions,
to slap a face and feel the sting. I want
the ground to meet me.

SUSAN'S DOLLS

She never believed the dolls slept
rather they came awake at night and sang and cried,
and loved and wished and dreamed and prayed for rain,
hair wild about their heads.
Saucy Walker strolled on the bed and Susan felt
the bedclothes tremble, but when she opened her eyes
the doll, as she was before, lay there still
and Monkey Doll jumped wide-grinned to the top
of the dresser and dangled all his limbs over the mirror
like some empty puppet.

But the most important waking came
when tiptoeing Tiny Tears across the window sill moved
under the moon, with all the reverence for the dead a doll
could muster, and then slowly, deliberately she cried
at first those small intermittent tears.
A great sob rose in her as she stared at Susan
beneath the covers;
the tears fell in torrents until the room was murky
with the floating limbs of dolls caught in the flood.

When the tears stopped and waters receded,
the bed that floated all night set itself down again.
The dolls pieced themselves together and sat,
heads bowed, hands folded,
and as they watched Susan's waking, not one of them dared
tell her how sad it is to think that only the living
know how to grieve.

The saddest part of any site destroyed
by nature's heavy hands or by mine,
if I begin to think too long, must be
the sudden naked glow of a doll's arm
parting the soil or riding a wave that leaves
the shore by night. There is this voice—the sound

like someone's mother calling; a pealing sound
in memory's chamber, long ago destroyed
and buried deep beneath the groan of leaves
that disapprove of dying. Inside me
there is the tug of winter that makes me arm
my youth against what will and will not be.

And if the plastic eyes appear to be
tearful—the cracked head kicked, no longer sound—
I have this urge to splint the broken arm
that waves goodbye, as if childhood—destroyed
and tossed aside—could be restored. To myself
I whisper, "I love you," hushed in the dust that leaves

me soiled with guilt. It is this dirt which leaves
its claim on me, reminds me I will be
forever looking back to find myself
in bits and pieces scattered amidst the sound
of a baby's cry, the present destroyed
and hanging on the maple that thrusts an arm

across twilight. Where is the cushioned arm
of father's chair, where daytime battle leaves
me? Where now the bedtime friend that destroyed
the rats beneath the springs, choosing to be
near the pillow to guard the ear from sound
and stroke a weary cheek? I am not myself

these days, having lost my toys to free myself
from weakness, thinking any puny arm
could cradle the sea. I was wrong to sound
out the syllables of strength so soon. Time leaves
me shipwrecked by prickly waves that must be
drowning the innocence I have destroyed.

Although destroyed, the past creeps toward me,
becomes the night's thief that I would disarm,
and leaves its haunting echo to choke all sound.

in her blue house her husband is dying
as we all are   but his hastens on
and we read our separate books

the tea is too hot to drink
and he rushes to the bathroom with an attack
of something—warns me when he returns
to wait awhile before using it   this
is the beginning and the end
of our conversation

strange evening, but beautifully quiet
here with this man I know little and
like even less   how is it that I can
not like him, even now

I've chosen a chair on the other side
of the living room   I do not dare sit
on the same sofa for fear he needs room to die
and I dare to stop reading, to write about him
as he just now shifts his weight and fixes his robe

(I remind myself of a story where
a man is pinned between a subway train
and a platform, dying and knowing it.
No one liked him either and all felt guilt,
all felt grief in his passing.)

we sit in distances far away from each other
perfectly contented with our own rates
of death   comforted with our own silent voices

my friend lingers late
as her husband and I read on

She died today before I could see her again.
I didn't know. I called to see if I could visit.
Your father told me. He said she always
loved me, this woman who took your part
even when you were wrong, who wanted you
to stay home until you married, who wanted
someone else to be your wife.

She cried once at one of my concerts.
It was during "And Then There Was You."
I remember softening then, but the hardness
returned when you married. I gloated
when you lost the election by thousands of votes.

A grieving woman at the funeral turned to me.
"How very nice of you to come," she said.
I was glad the partition hid you and your family.
The rabbi's eulogy was about a glorious woman,
a woman intensely happy that all her children
remained "married to their original spouses,
a woman who never got over her daughter's
death, a woman admired for her spiciness."
Who was she? I might have loved her.

Your new home sits alone in the valley you bought.
I'm told there are five-acre lots for sale around
you. Can't imagine seeing you and your wife
every day. In your valley your dreams will come true:
you will raise and sell your Christmas trees, have
your shooting range, collect your rents, grow your
children, come home to your wife.

You will always miss your mother more than
your wife, more than anyone. Hers will be the
voice coaxing you to do everything. You will
never know how I feel. You will only see me
from a distance, passing in and out of stores
in Oneida, stopped at a traffic light, crossing
Main Street by the bank.

PHOTO FINISH

I can see where doves could freeze on the bird bath if
they waited long enough, if they sensed
that in their haste they might
miss the beautiful hardness of water.

I can see where fear might extinguish their blue-flamed
hearts, drive them to the sky away
from rock that accepts the cold.

This urge to stay: the need to touch
a wing to its own reflection, to feel feather
stroke feather, watch beak peck beak
to know the instant when image is not image but real.

IN MY CLOSET THE BLACK-EYED ANGEL

rests in an array of silk
greys naturally and meditates daily

often her wings are broken
and she is like the lost soul
who resides in the painting
in my hallway, never wholly
transparent, occasionally
a mist in the closet when I
confront her, her leather sandals
unstrapped, body limp
in the morning

today she could be a bat in daylight
I imagine her body casts a shadow
on the wall
she could be my guardian
were she not weak from all her tears

She eats a nectarine and a stream of juice
falls from her chin. She is undaunted.
I need to listen to her. She continues to talk

about some woman years ago wheeling a baby carriage
up to the railroad crossing, and how one of those balls
that rose to lift the gate fell onto to the carriage and

missed the baby and how fortunate they both were.
When she reaches the pit she bites around it, fingers
dripping, lips puckered, so uninhibited and contented

I feel alone. And she starts another story about a man
caught on the same railroad track in his car and how
he died and what his family is like today. I forget

the details of this story too, seconds after she tells them.
I know only that I should savour what she says, the
        sound of
her voice telling me anything, her lips puckering like
        they

must have when she was a young girl. To know her
        somehow
and not feel alone. I need to listen to what she says.
To know her somehow and not feel alone.

FOUR

A GARDEN IN LAYERS —

a dream of phlox and cardinals
mourning doves mourning
skunks skunking, tiger lilies tigering

it borders a wire fence
and Jubay's shingled shed

a lone dogwood is wispy yet
and last year's geraniums love pink or red
sparrows dive-bomb the bird bath
composter looming in the distance, busy
growing mysterious things

it is August and the garden grieves
for faded flowers
almost moans with thoughts of autumn

*

and what about mother
there is no word for what has been lost

she could be in the garden
wearing white lace

she could be anywhere
smelling sweet and young
before her breakdown
when she was a fern, too green
to notice it hadn't rained,
that she hadn't quenched her thirst for happiness

*

near the grass
the deep dirt wanderings of ivy
cool white phlox

*

I descend the stairs of the deck
to sit in the midst
to be there
where it begins
where it reaches
toward the sky
sun on my legs, a quilt of light
pouring small fire into my veins

*

she could be a climber,
a trumpet vine carpeting
then rising above the ground,
orange vessels looking for hummingbirds

*

level with the bird bath
I try to imagine life
without you

*

chickadees:
minute splashes
tiny beating hearts that know nothing
about death
except how to avoid it

*

alone with my own voices
seen only by impatiens
staring out from hosta
phlox above it all

does my voice become my father's
from some grave that follows me here
his voice telling me he loves the man
I married
what can I tell myself when grief
meets me head-on again
and the garden sighs back at me
mutters that life lives only
where we plant it
sun or no sun
wet or dry

*

the woman in my tree
holds her hands on her chest
palms to breasts
soft inner bark beating

preserved, she stands
so that any lover may find her,
certain she will not feel
anything, cheeks burnt in the sun
toes curled up under rocks

*

the breeze may be all that the day needs
to lift itself off the ground

*

dear green, all the greens of the world
united to pull the grieving dead
from their silent houses
even so, you will shrivel with
my neglect

*

she could be moss that cushions my feet
springs back to life
and breathes beneath the dogwood.

NOTHING ISSUES FROM THE MORNING

the last angel hangs on the last branch;
I think it must cry—the angel, I mean.

I think it must let out all the mist
of its unused mercy.

it is no clearer the closer I get
but I know it will not rise again;

it is hanging there, hanged,
neck in a homemade sling

against the dark tree
against the light sky

hair white and damp and still
shoulders limp, fading.

I try untying the rope
lifting the body,

but it slips through my fingers.
I remember that too late.

my hands melt through the air
inside the image,

an angel with a broken neck no one
can fix.

ASCENSION

without knowing it

she found her way in the dark

hair loose and brown and damp

during August, when summer is heavy

when cicadas are louder than silence she suffered

more than the corpse she'd just seen, or the corpse she was,

she was grief, ice in spite of the heat, fog everywhere

inside her

they would have buried her

had it not been for the sudden breeze

in her wings

MY MOTHER'S VOICES

rain runs wild
down drainpipe ridges
flooding my heart

inside wet caves
my mother's voice
like dead leaves

when death looms
sure before us

the last god
loved my mother

all her voices
they grow louder
become the life

near Attleboro Castle
under God's light
with new knowledge
candles live somewhere

echoing, calling, asking
falling on shadows
light grows tall
large, and stands

some wind from

a black stone
tries to silence

the screams inside

she never had

                            a new god
                            begins to call
                            the names of

ancestors who knew
the same pain

                            the old gods
                            who never stopped loving

are ancestors who died

                            any god knows
                            that to live
                            is to sink deeper
                            into hope

hope always learns
to freeze rocks

                            when winter claims
                            the scarlet night

the end is all   there is

                  nothing

I see a child outside, alone and hurting still.
Susan stands just behind the hedge, her hair
a tangle of days. It is the constant wind
she chooses to befriend, a wind that breaks the glass
of her heart, a wind beyond all reason. Plants
uprooted, with forgotten names, belong to an age

when Susan was clothed and cared for, an age
when she remembers that love and food still
held their flavours, when the summer in her planted
all manner of living things, when gnarled hair
was the result of sleep, when shattered glass
meant only a replacement window. A new wind

uses her. Susan watches her own mother wind
a cord around a baby doll's neck—ageless
this feeling of betrayal when the glassy
eyes of some doll fill with rage and still
the end will not come. Her mother's hair
long now, takes root in the doll's fingers, planted

firmly in a grasp meant to be the final planting,
here in this building where death eludes the wind
temporarily—where nurses are too busy to brush hair,
a constant source of life, mother's hair, that ages
with time. She sits or stands in her room, still
hoping that Susan will pick the coloured glass

from both their broken hearts, and knows that glass
shattered will always be separate, knows that planting
anything in this home of ancient lovers cannot still
the anger, knows the winter descends with winds
stronger than any ability to mend. No amount of aging
produces a calm wind. And in this darkness, hair

continues to grow. Even after death, relentless hair
will lengthen. Susan moves closer to the window—glass
intact, loves her mother from outside, wants the age
of love to return, uses her hands to ready soil for planting,
prays that the ground will accept any gift, that winds
will subside, that underneath hair and glass there is still

a place where wind is kind, where fragile hands of age
touch youthful hands planted in the future, a place of glass
where hair is alive, where rage lies down and anger stills.

IT IS THE HANDS THAT MATTER,

the disposal of the uterus
and who stared into the darkness

the hands follow me everywhere
so much of me pushed aside, fondled

that I don't remember where I begin
only that the hands know what has become of me

this blood that leaves me
leaves me forever

there must be a vast river somewhere filled
with the stuff of me

and it never dries up or seeps into the ground
it only rolls on, spreads out

filling the landscape, surrounds the hedges
oozes from the rocks

begs space in the ditches
and leaves marks on the bark of trees

for I am many separate selves that wake under stars
and never recognize the moon

part of me washes up everywhere
and the night cannot console me

nothing reaches me
I abandon myself on every shore

even the hands have deserted me
and it is incredible that I wish for them.

PURPLE

Must be the colour of the heart's centre,
like Christ's robe in the picture on mother's
dresser, like the folds of the womb
that enclose each night.

It is the skin's passion
or spots on the sun or
velvet over stone when nothing
else will warm the torso of some

statue. And it leaves me blind after
the flash of the camera, drawn into the
dark, less likely to care if the sun rises,
more lonely than stillbirth

or no birth at all.

HOW TO DESTROY A COLOUR

You feel it in the voice of your dying mother
who tells you spring will never be
again. She stops eating. She kills herself
always in summer, when doing so bothers you
the most, when doing so makes you question
why green was ever invented.

How to destroy a colour. This dying
is constant. This voice descends everywhere
in whispers. It withers the ferns. You
are almost glad nothing green survives.

sighing to the afternoon, waiting for something
to join it. Another leaf falls. And like the notes
on a long scale, one by one the leaves drop out
of sight. Nothing lingers but their groaning.

This is not quite believable, their scoffing at me
who has never known such distance from myself.
I envy them, their crispness like nothing I have ever felt,
their very will to touch the ground and know

that by their touching they rekindle all the fire
they have lost. Not their frailness, only their approach
to death moves me. I would dig myself under
but for their possession of the ground. Leaves do not

relinquish what they cover. They await with patience their
descent into dust and I begin to see myself for the first
time, written there into the fabric of some leaf, its veins
my veins. And I think this is as it should be, one leaf

covering another, my dust indistinguishable from theirs.

THE LAST TREE

for W.S. Merwin

the ground awaits the impact of the last tree falling

when earth will receive it to its breast

when it will lodge there in the grass

and fester

not quite silent

the sound like the last beat of a tired heart

will echo somehow into the night

the wind won't be seen anymore

it will sigh

the muffled screams of ten thousand leaves

the wind will sigh

and we will wonder how something so strong

can be so thin

NOT TO BE FINISHED

this year this grieving
that shows itself at dusk
the same visitor but older now
well-worn and almost comfortable
like a coat I don to hold what's left of you
close to me, to warm me when no one listens
because I've told everyone too often
how I miss you.

when suppers linger on the stove
I wonder if you are
anywhere I am.
you seem to hover when I come home.

nothing ends like a day in November
when every leaf has fallen and you lie there
waiting for the snow again.

how unlike me

you are in death.

HEAVEN IS HEAVEN

because nothing ever
changes. it must be

a place where trees never
die, where roots dig deep

to fix the soil hard,
a place left intact

under the trunk of
some maple, a place

safe in sun, where
light lingers, and the

moon is always full,
where the only season

is the length of shadow.

FIVE

BALLOON

This fine yellow balloon tossed on the breeze
lands where green tries but cannot swallow it,

throws itself again and again into the air,
wanting more of everything

and certainly more air
as if there could never be enough air outside or in.

It calls me to it somehow
though I am almost out of sight.

It wants me, pulls me toward it,
needs me on the inside, nose flattened.

We rise over my house
my car like some toy to me now,

everything yellow, even children
who begin to disappear,

the trees like faded broccoli,
the roads, lines on a map with no direction.

First ponds, then lakes and oceans, come into view
and evaporate.

I breathe harder, inhale rubber,
fill the sky with longing.

There is little I can tell you about dirigibles—
little about contents, sailability, mechanics, economy.
Little to be said about occupancy or engine sound,
no images from experience, few from photos or feeling.
No memories from a vacation or afternoon lift,
only knowledge learned from old film and current

football games. Imagination is a cloud on air currents
that floats just above the trees, a sentient balloon
in a sunset sky, no strings attached, lightly lifted
by waves of thought, inspired by the economics
of silent space. It moves with the air, feels
free from the shackles of restless wind, sounds

more and more like love. If memory resounds
in me, there truly is some sense that current
longings for the past place me close enough to feel
the loss of the Hindenburg, the terror of the airship's
demise, a reporter's lamentations, his lack of economy
in expressing his shock. Maybe I remember, lift

my Jameson in honour of open grief. What else can lift
itself away from that recollection? Let's pretend sound
died with death, that no one worried about the economics
of loss, that breath left easily and took with it all current
memory of this event. The present is left with an air bus
that regains its grace, and remembrance suddenly feels

good again. Sun glints off the surface of feeling.
Blue jays chuckle at *big bird* above them and lift
themselves higher in friendly competition. *Blimp*
becomes the word for mother in a soundless
twilight when ground feeders collect currants
and look up in awe at a passing shadow. Economy

means nothing when air is a floating miracle. Economy
disappears. Night is only a darker shade of day, feeling
is a black whisper, and breath a velvet current.
Imagine an oval filled with air, an effortless shape lifted
as far away as time allows, farther than sound's
report. Imagine one of every species and race, on a ship

never bound to feel the end of searching—where sound
advice is economy of language: *go, live, love, lift*—
you in the Zeppelin there, taming the air of all currents.

An out-of-town patron looks for comfort here
or anywhere in the park in Clinton
and listens to trucks around the circle grind their brakes.
When they are gone the birds resume
their questioning of the sun and no one
knows her here, or ever will. This is strange
and beautiful.

The village cop circles again and wonders how
someone can write so much. Something wonderful
about a cool breeze in summer that she knows
will turn warm. Such a sure thing
that there can be no sadness in it
no hope of despair.

Nothing ever changes.
Even the bare spaces where trees stood
have given up their secrets and she
is not confused by them. New storefronts
are only coverings and she remembers what lies
underneath. And concrete, simply a facade over dust,
has not changed the earth under it.
No ability anywhere knows how to change.

She knows suddenly that time never passes,
always simply endures and us with it—
though aging never aged,
though young never born—
only always potentially here or there.
And being here she wonders how anything ever
descends.

She knows now she moves diagonally
(and that is the mystery)
along a fine line of sunlight at the edge of the park
and that sitting here could be sitting anywhere
so displaced is she. And space
does not exist except where
she places it

and she places herself seated or standing anywhere
on feet that could be anyone's.
Not black or white or pink
they just are
and they stand and do not know they stand
and walk and do not know they walk.
It is not likely they ever arrive
only that they move somehow,
but never over the same pavement twice.
Tomorrow which does not exist
never comes.

Everyone is moving, the train
thrusting them toward the next platform
and I sit crying until you lean over
and say: *They're going to think I'm beating you.*

I laugh at this, then more tears as the train
pushes forward again and people scramble
in their city pace, defying the doors to close
before they can squeeze through.

> I remember the B&B in Stratford
> where the lady stroked your beard and said
> *He's lovely, isn't he?* and I said yes
> a thousand times to myself; the nights
> on our honeymoon when we were stationary
> in small towns and love by you was never fast
> but slow and safe.

On Dundas, in a tiny consignment shop, I wait
for you inside someone else's jacket. In a
corner facing the street I wrap my arms around
me, stand still, imagine you are holding me—
keeping me safe, unmoving, blocks away from
the subway.

HOT AND SOUR SOUP ON SPADINA

orgasm of senses
leaping against soft cheek walls
green onions surfing the teeth
black bean pork broth floating my tongue
pepper exploring nasal cavities

I speak no speak—look at my husband
who has tasted all this before

but the soup, only the soup—
brown, spicy-hot and heated—
goes through my head, becomes
a mind of its own

 my drug of choice again and again

breathless, exhausted after all, nameless

imagine the liquid descending
toward organs that loosen, my own
WD-40, full massage with each
swallow

I was born for this—taste of
August sun, bracing for autumn!

WHEN YOU KISSED ME

you told me
not to leave my eyes

open, that it bothered you to know
I was seeing what you could not,

but I am your eyewitness
and I remember kissing the crease

of your silent eye and thinking:
when two skins touch,

the air that holds them distant
is no more.

SKETCHING IN WARREN, MICHIGAN

I draw a black outline, my hand trembling
    as I round his buttocks with smooth lines.

It is too round, some deformed offspring
    of my fear of imperfection. Sight blinds

me, for I miss the curve of his calf
    when I look ahead to his pink heel,

charcoal choking the page, running off
    the sketch pad before his toes can tell

of their existence. "Start with weight," Jane says.
    "Start with something other than the head.

The head does not express the feelings — the phase
    of emotion." I start again — use a lead

pencil to stroke his dark thigh — hard
    and round and ready to be where the weight

is centred. Again the curve eludes me, hears
    me coming, moves away from my sight,

sliding under my line as Robin's muscle
    rolls and I am caught by his shadowed beauty —

by night in all its landscape, it full-
    ness, its rare and subtle nudity.

BEYOND SLEEP

Bent double, like old beggars under sacks,
Knock-kneed, coughing like hags, we cursed through sludge,
Till on the haunting flares we turned our backs,
And towards our distant rest began to trudge.

"Dulce et Decorum Est," Wilfred Owen

There are no trees in my long yard.
They exist just beyond the linked
fence that holds my garden back
from my neighbours'. Rude oaks laugh
at maples from opposite sides of lawn,
their crispy leaves filled with cracks.
It takes twenty bags, packed hard
to clear the land in autumn — twenty bags
piled curbside each November, our backs
bent double, like old beggars under sacks,

cringing from the weight of them. Yet
the shadows from summer branches
speak to us like whispering angels
between June and September. Our skin
dances with lacy patterns, our smooth
foreheads cooled and safe; we don't judge
trees then, rather we silently worship them
while sitting and dreaming of darkness
and fresh earth teeming with worms. No grudge.
Knock-kneed, coughing like hags we curse through sludge

in October. I imagine light is told
to breathe freely, to exhale with all its
brilliance, leaving us raw and bruised
with too much colour; imagine fire within us,
the growing embers of our hearts, our
pathetic, blistered feet and bloodied tracks
in our futile attempts to escape; see
the burning bush next door burn before autumn,
shoot flames towards sunset, branches bursting flak,
till on the haunting flares we turn our backs

and all our longing returns with night, its cloak
of black. With thanks we remember it takes
only a season to forget ourselves, only one
winter nodding into spring to remind us:
leaves fall freely as we recover all we're
meant to be, that trees descend to nudge us
into action before earth can sleep again,
before death lays its weary head on winter's lap.
We force ourselves beyond the days that judge us
and towards our distant rest begin to trudge.

ARQUINT ROAD

the descent is all that matters

the crickets, the forward motion down

the descent in the dark after rain.

left alone in the night the fog falls

like some great, floating bird

feathers everywhere

even inside the car.

drive faster, push harder

listen to quiet farms

and the eternal trees.

nothing matters as long as

when you get there the columbines

are blooming, like tremendous little hats,

the lupines never so lush so early.

FINALLY A MOMENT

when green as never before stands tall
and the sun
pours something other than light down
here where sitting is new
where stones stop screaming
time answers nothing

it is in the field beyond the grey car
between Alvord's garden and me
that some red rose asks
how long

some list in my head
counts the wounds that have
the most wonderful scars

often I know less
about the stones or the evening
less about the breeze that is
never the same

NOTES & ACKNOWLEDGEMENTS

The Italics in "After Summer" (pg. 18) are from the poem "Summer" by Laura Lush.

Some of the poems in this book first appeared, sometimes in earlier versions or with different titles, in the following publications:

Transversions, Blueline, Four Quartets, Poetpourri, The Comstock Review, Southern Poetry Review, Kalliope, Lake Effect, Lullwater Review, The Georgia Review, Feminist Studies, Yankee, Footwork, Northwords, 5 A.M., *Hubbub, The Antigonish Review, TickleAce, Negative Capability.*

Some of the poems were previously published in the chapbook *Water Voices* (Junction Books, 2000).

"On 'The Red Soil'" won the Daniel Varoujan Award in 1998.

"Waiting for the Bookstore to Open" won the first annual Milton Dorfman prize in 1990.

§

Special thanks to the following people: Molly Peacock for her guidance with the first version of this book; Adrienne Weiss for her skill in editing the final version; Carleton Wilson and Junction Books for constant support of my work, and Silas White of Nightwood Editions; Al Moritz and the Algonquin Square Table poets for their help with many of these poems; Michael Burkard, who taught me about freedom; Jennifer B. MacPherson; Gayle Elen Harvey; Frank Bjornson; my dear parents; and my dear husband, Michael Glicksohn, who is my patient listener.

Trish Skrypchyk

ABOUT THE AUTHOR

Susan Manchester has lived most of her life in central New York State, moving to Toronto in 1993. She has taught high school English for twenty-five years and has also been an instructor at the State University of New York at Morrisville and at Utica College of Syracuse University. Her poems have appeared in *The Georgia Review, The League of Canadian Poets Anthology, Tesseracts 8, The Antigonish Review*, as well as many others. Poetry awards to her credit include the Summer Sizzler Poetry Contest (*Poetpourri*), the Milton Dorfman Award and the Daniel Varoujan Prize. She divides her time between teaching English at Etobicoke Collegiate Institute, acrylic painting, writing and singing.

A Junction Book

Typeset in TEFF Collis

Designed in 1993 by Christoph Noordzij for The Enschedé
Font Foundry.

Printed and bound in Canada

EDITOR
Adrienne Weiss

EDITOR FOR THE PRESS
Carleton Wilson

COPY EDITOR
A.J. Levin

TYPESETTING
Carleton Wilson

COVER DESIGN
Tim Franz

COVER PHOTOGRAPH
"Venus Dawn," Jim Thibert

Junction Books
568 Indian Grove · Toronto, ON · M6P 2J4
www.junctionbooks.com

Nightwood Editions
www.nightwoodeditions.com